AMERICA'S FAVORITE POEM

Also by Jason Koo

Poetry
More Than Mere Light
Man on Extremely Small Island

As Coeditor
Brooklyn Poets Anthology

AMERICA'S FAVORITE POEM

JASON KOO

BROOKLYN ARTS PRESS
BROOKLYN, NY

America's Favorite Poem
Copyright © 2014 by Jason Koo

ISBN: 978-1-936767-62-5

Cover design: Trent Thibodeaux
Cover photo: Jason Koo

All rights reserved. No part of this publication may be reproduced by any means existing or to be developed in the future without written consent by the publisher.

Published & Printed in the United States of America by:
Brooklyn Arts Press
154 N 9th St #1
Brooklyn, NY 11249
www.BrooklynArtsPress.com
info@BrooklynArtsPress.com

First BAP Edition, 2020.
Originally published by C&R Press, 2014.

Distributed to the trade by Small Press Distribution / SPD
www.spdbooks.org

for Anna Greenberg

CONTENTS

AMERICAN DREAM	3

I

A NATURAL HISTORY OF MY NAME	7
GIANT STEPS	9
AMERICA'S FAVORITE POEM	12
TAKE YOUR TIME	14
GQ CORRESPONDENCE	16
STRUCK FROM THE FLOAT FOREVER HELD IN SOLUTION	17
SENT DAD A GOLF TRUNK ORGANIZER	20
EMPTY ORCHESTRA	22
FOR EVERY ATOM BELONGING TO ME	25
MODEL MINORITY	26
SOMETIME SWEEP	30
IN PASSING WITH MY MIND ON NOTHING IN THE WORLD BUT THE RIGHT OF WAY I ENJOY BY VIRTUE OF THE LAW	34
TO LEBRON'S ELBOW	35
CONTENTS TEND TO SHIFT DURING FLIGHT	39

II

SELF-INSTALLATION	45
WHAT WE TALK ABOUT WHEN WE TALK ABOUT	46
LUNCH SPECIAL	48
ORPHEUS ON LEXINGTON AVENUE	51
FIRST SONG	52
THE FUTURE ROOM	54
THE SOUND	56
CLOSE EMBRACE	58
I'LL FOLLOW YOU	64
EMPIRE	65
THE CONTINUING STRUGGLE OF THE PHILISTINES JR.	68
HERE ARE YOUR WATERS AND YOUR WATERING PLACE	71
KISSING YOU	72
WORK	77

Just needed time alone with my own thoughts
Got treasures in my mind but couldn't open up my own vault
My childlike creativity, purity and honesty
Is honestly being crowded by these grown thoughts
Reality is catchin' up with me
Takin' my inner child, I'm fightin' for it, custody
With these responsibilities that they entrusted me
As I look down at my diamond-encrusted piece

—Kanye West

AMERICAN DREAM

after Shakespeare 129

Had, having, and in quest to have, extreme.
What's the point of being ridiculous?
Over and over and over again, it seems.

Enough's enough, enough to make you scream.
Well, you don't. You're quiet. Meticulous.
Had, having, and in quest to have, extreme.

You browse through dirty thumbnails on a screen
Then click Clear History, recoil in disgust.
Over and over and over again, it seems.

This gives new meaning to the phrase *come clean*.
A silly sully-cycle—you're into this?
Had, having, and in quest to have, extreme?

Not a human being but an in-between,
There, not there, there and not there, more or less
Over and over and over again, it seems.

Oh Mister Umpteen, Mixmaster Misqueme,
What's the point of being ridiculous?
Had, having, and in quest to have, extreme.
Over and over and over again you dream.

I

A NATURAL HISTORY OF MY NAME

after Google

Today I read that only 2.2%
    out of a million first and last names
have a higher vowel than consonant ratio,
    and, since 50% of the letters
in my name are vowels, this means
    I am "extremely well envoweled."
I go outside strutting the bulge
    in my name: the trees are wowed
by my vowels, they only have two e's,
    which is why they have no leaves
at this time of year: the snow must submit
    to the scrunch of my boots,
snow only has one o and I have three,
    even my boots, so tough and rugged,
clearly dominating the one-o'd
    snow, must bow down to the deity
of me, with three, never raising
    themselves higher than my feet:

I cross the bridge and it is the same,
    the river cannot keep up
with me, look at it writhing in the ice,
    so fearsome with its 66.7%
envowelment but not so
    intimidating to me, because ice,
if you'll notice, slides on its c,
    eventually skidding to a stop
like a hockey player before the puck
    of the e: which in a flick
disappears: whereas I keep floating out
    on my opening of o's, the song

of my name is repeated through nature,
    cuckoos and owls take pleasure
in perpetuating it, just one koo
    is never enough for them, koo
must always come coupling

    through their throats: you can hear
this song taken up by schoolchildren,
    I used to hear it all the time,
I thought kids were taunting me
    but now I know they were just jealous
of my o's: they saw these heaped
    in their bowls of canned
spaghetti and cereal, but no matter
    how many spoonfuls they jammed
in their mouths, no matter how
    many more muscles they grew
than me, they never grew any
    more richly envoweled: this was just
something you had to be born with,
    a natural advantage of hailing
from a family that came from a tiny
    Pacific peninsula whupped
by other countries: our name shed
    contours of consonants
to slip past detection, shape-shifting
    into other words like a
syllable chameleon, from haiku to coup
    d'état matching colonial culture
and upheaval, so when I hear Hi Koo

    today followed by a giggle,
the laugh is not on me but on the oppressors,
    whose whole poetic tradition
gets wiped out by my arrival.

GIANT STEPS

for Gunny Scarfo

I'm listening to Tommy Flanagan and thinking of the quality
That separates great artists from mediocre ones: tenderness, taste, charm,
    gravity, light—
But are you capable of some mean-ass fucking?
Tommy Flanagan, I'll admit, I was skeptical when I bought your tribute
    album for John Coltrane,
Thinking you had some Giant Steps to fill,
But you, Mraz and Foster just *kill*
"Mr. P. C.," doing all kinds of nasty things to my cochlea, loosening my head
    at the hinge,
Saying, Henceforth thou shalt never associate the name Flanagan
With lovely, tasteful dinner-time ballads,
The kind you put on when a woman comes over for your prefab middle-
    class cooking—
I am not an ingredient in your four-course seduction meal,
I am not a twinkly Oscar Peterson background,
I am the author here, I will do you and do you and do you until I'm done.
Point taken, Mr. Flanagan,
I can scarcely understand how you're getting all this sound out of the piano,
You're just pounding away at me, what power!
(Scarcely? Stop saying scarcely!)
I want this power in an artist: I hate this new breed of poets
Who hate the word, the idea of power, favoring
Shriveled, dribbly productions, no chance of offending anybody, no chance
    of not getting tenure,
And meanwhile, as Mayakovsky says, the tongueless street writhes
For lack of something to shout or say.
I went to Times Square for a Poetry Society of America reading,
Wanting to hear something to match that massive, Moby-Dickian energy,
To put all that commerce in its place, Sephora, Billabong, MTV,
To outlava the panoramic magma of ads,

But all I got were cool susurrations, poets barely able
To muster a look at themselves in the Jumbotron projecting them,
As if to do so would be egotistical, surely the worst sin in poetry since Keats,
No one wants to offend Keats! And no, no ego here,
None of these poets tried to publish or entered this Times Square Alliance/PSA contest or built up their bios,
They were just happy to be here,
Or not be here, manifesting their Negative Capability and leaving it to the people behind them
To stop and look at themselves in the Panasonic mirror:
People who'd never seen themselves
So glorious, laughing and making faces and capturing themselves
On digital camera, calling up friends and family members on cell phones to share their dwindling minutes
Of fame: one suited man, looking a little like the towering Jay Z
In the Rocawear billboard above us, anchored himself
Behind the poets in the center of the Jumbotron, brushing away the gnats of their faces
From his face, the true subject
Of the true new poem of America, assembling ominously
Behind the jigsawed pieces the professional poets were gingerly inching together:
As if he'd found his final home, arriving at total peace
Within his own vanity, not self-conscious at all about staring at himself for an hour,
And I had to admit, there was something impressive in this,
The way he so blatantly broadcast his own self-adoration
Unlike the poets reading, one of whom, my friend, called the people "disgusting,"
Or me, who wanted to be up there in place of them, thinking I could
Blow people off the block with my Big Verse,
Already imagining the poem I would enter in the PSA contest the next year,
But who after the reading just told everybody nice job
And went along for the free fancy dinner and stayed in the friend's free fancy hotel room,
Not bursting out of that bullshit, imagining I was better than everyone else
But acting self-effacing, thinking this would earn me points,
Not yet capable of the elevation

That could make that crowd go wild with something other
Than themselves, something Jay Z would've smacked into them in a second:
I'm in the hall already, on the wall already, I'm a work of art, I'm a Warhol already:
    yeah, motherfuckers,
It takes a real ego
To destroy the sense of ego, something all mean-ass fucking Flanagans understand.

AMERICA'S FAVORITE POEM

> *In this country there is a universal third person,*
> *the man we all want to be.*
>   —Don DeLillo

I'm dreaming of myself in the universal third person,
 floating through Target and seeing drawers full of soft white
Merona cotton tees. Or maybe Calvin Klein, $2^{(x)}$ist—
 to exist means raising your life to the power of product x.
Sage green shower poufs. Striped FLOR modular carpet tiles.
 The expenses disappear into far-flung credit card orbits
where the moons are APRs. Let's order sleek black Chelsea boots

 by Hugo Boss, $298 but excusable after months of browsing
catatonic in the office on Zappos.com. Brown boots
 with snakelike stitching down the leather upper by Ben Sherman
and ooh, look, with purchase receive a kickass canvas
 drawstring bag that solves the problem of how to fly
with a wardrobe that necessitates both brown and black footwear.
 Messenger bag by Manhattan Portage. Watch by Omega.

Okay maybe not Omega. But to be able to fill that supreme
 confidence of Daniel Craig's Bond in *Casino Royale*, to say, when
asked about the gorgeous timepiece on his wrist, "Rolex?"
 "Omega." The confidence capped by a single branded word.
Custom-made tux by Brioni. Turnbull & Asser shirt.
 This man walks on shoes built like Jaguars, sports a different watch
for every occasion. Black Victorinox Swiss Army watch

 for bathing on a Brazilian beach in a soft grey Bottega Veneta
T-shirt ($220) next to a bronzed, razorboned siren
 wearing only a string-knotted bikini bottom by Melissa Odabash
as she arches back over a boulder like the leather strap
 of a watch, flattening her breasts with one arm

and staring off into the oystered, Odysseus-laden horizon.
    Classic Cartier with a thin black alligator strap for the October

wedding. He has a box to store his watches, tie bars, cuff links.
    The box itself costs as much as the jewelry it contains.
This man has wicked white sneakers designed by Common Projects
    with nothing on them but the serial no. of the manufacturer.
He wears the sneakers in the summer with fine white pinstripe khakis
    not by Banana Republic. He has the crotch of his pants
tailored to cup his package right. He has a tailor he can trust.

    A tailor he need not tell what to do, who makes *suggestions*.
A female tailor with strongly sculpted calves and yoga contour
    to her shoulders. Who looks fantastic in a business skirt
and sleeveless blouse. Who fucks him on a Tuesday-Thursday afternoon
    lecture-course schedule. In the dressing room,
of course. This man does not have skin problems. He sees
    a dermatologist named Wolfe who takes a single seasoned look

at his dry skin issues and solves them without having to take
    a small skin sample the size of a fingernail. Who does not prescribe
a steroid foam that runs out after a week and only aggravates
    the problem. This man fucks the PA with the fabulous thighs
to punish her for making faulty prescriptions. She knows nothing
    about dermatology but who cares? As long as he's getting less
than lugubrious sex for his copay. This man does not watch *The Notebook*

    four times in one day because he's in an emotional coma.
He finds Rachel McAdams soothing, but in the way
    a nice Chesterfield coat is soothing, one night of the year
and no more. She is not the answer to all his life's problems.
    He has no "problems." He stays in motion, attacking potential
problems like bicycle pedals that propel him forward.
    His life does not depend upon the addition of this blender.

TAKE YOUR TIME

>2008. A large circular mirror affixed to the
>ceiling at an angle rotates slowly on its axis,
>destabilizing your perception of space.

I'm not seeing this, staring up at the sky
Of myself, barely noticing the others

Scattered around me, or should I say
In me, happy to be free to look at myself

In public without pause, without self-
Consciousness, without having to act like I

Am actually considering buying a mirror
As I have done in the mirror aisle at Target:

Impossible to judge how you really look
Within the climate control of your own home,

So how nice to be able to study myself
In such institutional relief, PS1 vacuum-

Sealing the vanity out of my experience
And making it culturally pristine, stamped

With the Ólafur Elíasson imprimatur, a name
I'm pronouncing in all its permutations

In my head so I can drop it authoritatively
To friends, who hopefully won't correct me:

I check how closely I match the construction
I drew up, that sunny, relaxed Italian look

I was going for with this new white linen shirt,
These khakis, which earlier, at the MoMA,

In a narrower mirror installation, had looked
Too trim, but now, against the floor, projected

With such Sistine eminence, drape perfectly
Over my body, making me want to lie on

This floor forever—or long enough to net
A cool profile photo—basking in my Vitruvian

Ascension: I wonder if the artist meant this
As a joke, knowing we'd take this time

To "destabilize our perception of space"
By adoring ourselves and excusing it as "art":

Meanwhile we're all flopping on the floor
Preening and taking pictures of ourselves,

Part of a larger, smarter installation, a diorama
On narcissism, on view to anyone passing

In the hall strong enough to resist the temptation
To join us: but no one's passing, everyone's

Coming in and looking up, no one wants to be
Left out of looking up, though this keeps us

Flattened on the floor, the mirror hovering
Like a UFO, allowing us to take our time

Taking our lives, not even needing to attack us,
Just letting us grow docile out of vanity.

GQ CORRESPONDENCE

Ass of the past is something nice to think about

Strolling down an autumn street in a nasty two-button tweed

Finger your argyle sweater to point out the fine

Complement you make to the pattern of falling leaves

The maple leaf is the best piece of autumn of the past

50 years and serves as an excellent emergency pocket square

We suggest the Paul Smith maple leaf square for $495

Or the BR Monogram for $75 or just pick up a leaf

Ass is accrued by properly tending to your belt buckle

Which should create a picture frame for the waist

Never make your crotch the Axis of Cheeseball

As we are fond of calling the style of Kim Jong Il

Calvin Klein is responsible for the most revolutionary underwear ads

Of the past 50 years just as Marky Mark is responsible for the most fitting

Book dedication: "I wanna dedicate this book to my dick"

STRUCK FROM THE FLOAT FOREVER HELD IN SOLUTION

Scuzzbuckets, my thanks.
You kicked me out of comfort and showed me how
Comfort was conniving to make me content
With an almost life, the life I sort of wanted to have.
And now I'm blasted out of sort of into the sun
Tonnage of this city. Look at the Bridge accelerating against the sky, taunting the tourists
With their tiny cameras
On the puny pier. It dares me to think of it
As a mere amenity, though this was the life
Ever since I first read Hart Crane and saw him on the roof of 110 Columbia Heights
Boasting the Brooklyn Bridge as his background.
He came with nothing and left buildings.
I came, even reduced by you, with much more
And walk around his old neighborhood
Like it's my inheritance. I walk past 110 Columbia Heights,
Where a Jehovah's Witnesses building now stands.
I see through their Watchtower to Crane's Broken Tower.
Out of the rubble of his life
Just one phrase's *swift unfractioned idiom* annihilates their literature.

I look down at the gleaming musculature
Of the East River and imagine Whitman curious in the crowd on Robert Fulton's Ferry
Imagining me. Did he imagine me, most particular me,
The only son of Korean immigrant parents, crossing with the others on the ferry?
I don't think I would have occurred
To him, which is no offense, as even the Brooklyn Bridge did not occur to him.
You could say Roebling, and then Crane, out-imagined Whitman,
But he had the right, the original idea.
And you can still feel his presence, my enemies, in the movement of these waters,
The generosity of his imagination rippling to me
Not banked by its limits, the kind of generosity you did not extend to me

As you imagined my life going nowhere.
I try to extend this generosity to you, shamed by Whitman
Into questioning my enjoyment of the view
On this gentrified shore, the reward for what I've done.
I could say I'm not as bad as you think, but it's true: I'm worse than you think.

Whitman knew this, knew *what it was to be evil*,
How we shouldn't be fooled by any soaring, generous spirit, least of all his,
That there was always something evil in it,
Always something conquering in the creative.
That Bridge up there, Crane's connective tissue, grand Gateway to the West,
Has evil in it, so many *dark patches* went into it, so many lives, quite literally, went into it,
John Roebling killed by it, Washington Roebling crippled by it,
Confined during construction to the same room
On Columbia Heights that Crane occupied as he climbed the Bridge with his own construction
And was killed by it. But his name is now an aria out of it,
His dark life made it leap with more life, just as Whitman's life made Fulton's Ferry
More lasting than a commute
Even after the Roeblings' Bridge replaced it
With this refurbished historic pier, where Whitman's words have washed up
To decorate the railings.

And now I'm enjoying the sculpted shade
Reading *East Goes West* by Younghill Kang, the heroic father of Korean American literature
Who made his share of enemies when he left his family behind
During the Japanese occupation of Korea, first to study Western science in Japan
By passing himself off as Japanese, then to flee to New York
Looking for that same rebirth, that *ever-revivified life*
That Crane sought, but *inexorably unfamiliar*, rebuffed by realities Crane never had to deal with,
Scuffling through a missionary college for a year in Canada
Reading *David Copperfield* out loud to his tutor

To gain better command of English, enough to write the first novels in the language
By a Korean in America. Kang surely imagined me.
He would be proud, I think, to see me living as a poet in Brooklyn Heights,
A part of his legacy, reading his book.
I'm feeling all of them, Whitman, Kang, Crane, move through me,
Wondering how I got so lucky to live in a precinct of their imagination
Then remembering that it was you, my enemies, who got me here, I had to be
    a little bad
For that to happen, so much good has come of such bad
That I can't help but worry, don't worry,
Whether I deserve it, whether I'm not the worst kind of American,
Whether I'll ever do enough to return what you gave me,
Whether I'll screw this up, whether I'll ever feel like I have enough,

Whether I am enough.

SENT DAD A GOLF TRUNK ORGANIZER

Every day I keep filling my notebook with lists. Laundry.
    Email. Deposit checks. Hand soap. Return address labels.
Travel shave foam. I make little bullet points with my pen
    and try to keep the bullets straight down the page.

Then I put a line through and a check mark next to each item
    as I accomplish it, as if to convince myself it were done.
Can one fill with blankness? Try emptied of fullness.
    Always something left to accomplish, as lists spawn

more lists and are potentially infinite, with nothing to cap
    their form, like a couplet. Just now I made a list
that begins, No more lists! Then I realized that was the end
    and put a line through and a check mark next to it.

More troubling, though, is the sense that these lists
    are my attempt to create a feeling of accomplishment
where no accomplishment is—not even a feeling, tadpoles
    of feeling, far from a full frog; and thus I wriggle

instead of building up the frog hops that could get me
    from pad to pad meditating on frog matters, surely more
interesting than tadpole trivialities, including things like
    the taste of flies and the feel of air and rain and the ramification

of water—and I could wield that whiplash of tongue
    like a lyric weapon in the bog. How is it with you, my self,
when you've gotten so low you're thinking through a frog?
    Sent dad a golf trunk organizer? Peed a little by the window?

That was supposed to read, "Read a little by the window."
    I am listing things in the past now, though this list is broken
all over my notebook—Get a list trunk organizer—
    so leafing through it is like finding little pieces of myself

crumbled off from where a tire had smashed through
     and left me printed zigzagged cracking on the ground.
I don't know where I am. And in the eyes of my friends,
     a flicker of difference, as if they long for the days

when they didn't have to talk to such well-pressed debris.
     I can see it in them, too, the crumbling of the best version
of themselves they'd planned, the work of themselves
     neglected, no longer approached as a daily problem,

so that we're all left sitting around vaguely thinking
     there's some kind of problem, when the problem is that
there is no problem, we don't see ourselves as problems,
     we've relaxed the math. Trash bags. Vacuum. Soup.

EMPTY ORCHESTRA

    More and more your memories
        of having fun turn into memories of you
being insufferable.
    You did what *you* wanted,

    singing Bon Jovi in the karaoke room
        while your best friend slumped over the song
book and your girlfriend stared
    in amazement from across the room,

    wondering, Who is this *guy?*
        as you pointed at her and sang, *We've gotta hold on
to what we've got* in a voice
    that can only be described as terrible,

    and the small Korean man
        brought the soju bottles and arranged them
artfully along the long table
    around which knees were politely

    avoiding any facial expression,
        except yours, which were squinting under the strain
of all that falsetto and the raw Japanese
    denim you'd been crushing them into

    day after day, trying to hone
        your sleek, ideal, repeatable shape, you, you,
look at how thick and glossy
    my you, your hands sang

as you petted your knees on the subway
and imagined they were looking more like
Roger Federer's knees,
which look so good in shorts,

you liked to say, Federer is the only man
who looks good in shorts, you liked to expound,
and you wore these comments
like your jeans, which is to say,

everyone else had to wear them
as much as you, taking on your singularity
and shining it back
like so many model moons, and, as any moon

can tell you, it is one thing to shine
back real light and another to boomerang knees
and denim, who's not going to
resent that, especially under the strain

of weightlessness. You feel the weight
now of all the ways you've been unfeeling, the little,
nameless, unremembered acts
of blindness and self-love that have

slid this distance between you
and your friends, worn down the once bright image
of you they had when you were
younger, the ballroom self baring

its bathrooms and closets, its cranky
janitorial staff, and while the self, you know,
is difficult to pin down,
flowing somewhere between

ballroom and bathroom, you're sure
      the weight of it is the weight of all those little acts,
how they've piled up
    and left an imprint on your friends,

    something a little sunken
      in how they regard you, singing and making
a fool of yourself, jumping up
    and spilling soju on the knees of the girl

    who's the only reason your best friend
      stuck around, so that at the end of the night
he ends up stuck
    holding your stuff in the elevator

    on the way down, and when
      you stir from your drunken half-sleep to shout,
Where is my bag?
    he gets to assure you, I got it.

FOR EVERY ATOM BELONGING TO ME

Sure, now you can walk, hold in your hand
a spoon, a ball, a book; bite into a carrot,
nicking the tip cleanly into your mouth;
piss drunk into a urinal, shifting like penguins
waddling through huge blue districts of ice;
swear at your mother, God, a football team;
swagger with self, the center of a sphere,
needing no help, bold-molten on your own.

But once you were nothing. All you ate was milk.
You spent your days wriggling on your back,
your head so heavy it pinned you to the floor.
Your mother picked you up, held you, helped you,
you can't imagine how much she helped you,
how much tenderness buoyed you from the start.

MODEL MINORITY

I was thinking on the subway yesterday and thinking I think this fairly
Frequently, *Fuhhhck* these people...

That's just a terrible tie.

Those two mayonnaised over that whole swath of bench where four people
    could fit,

Or six slim Asians.

I make myself into as tight an Asian as possible in crowds
As a courtesy to other people—

It's the model minority in me, you might say,
Coolly, while enjoying your extra space.

People move on me like a magnet: I'll be walking down the street
With a clear path in front of me

When someone ahead to my left swerves into my space.

Once in a hurry to Penn Station I tried to move past a young kid with my
    roller bag

And he *kicked* the bag, sending it into the stomach
Of a woman walking towards us.

Of course I apologized to the woman, who looked at me
As if it were my fault,

Then ran after the kid, after first gently repositioning
The wheels of my bag on the pavement,

Of course I didn't "run," I walked briskly in a straight line wheeling
My bag behind me,

And when I caught up to the kid I walked alongside him and said, That was not cool, sir.

I have no idea where that "sir" came from.

I might as well have said, That was a lovely ball, an excellent first touch.

The kid just looked me over and said, Fuck you, you fucking Chinese—
And stopped, thinking that was insult enough.

It's funny,

When I'm feeling sorry for myself
After something like this, my default comfort food is Chinese.

Not "good" or "real" Chinese,
But fucking Chinese, the General Tso's Chicken I've had

Photoclumped from state to state, the Chicken Lo Mein
Flaplocked in its warm white cardboard carton,

The Garlic Chicken with Rice I know by now

Should be renamed Garlic Broccoli Carrots Peas Onions Green Peppers Mushrooms Baby Corn & Chicken with Rice,

So minor a role does the chicken play in this dish.

Menus should indicate it comes in two volumes:
Vol. 1 for dinner, Vol. 2 microwaved for lunch the next day.

A curious feeling I have

Sitting down for Vol. 2 of General Tso's Chicken, how removed I am

Yet somehow *in* those mutilated morsels, blasted beyond recognition

Yet somehow more recognizable for that, not even
Not even real Chinese food, just as I'm not even

Not even fucking Chinese, as I said to that kid, or thought I said, or thought
    to that kid

After he kicked my bag and left me to contemplate

Serious violence only while waiting in line later for the bus with my girlfriend,

Who sympathized at first but decided I was being unpleasant, I could tell,
The more I mowed

Over the story, the more incredulous I got at what the kid had done.

Who is this whose grief bears such an emphasis?

I was not playing the role she liked, the role I'm happy

To step into late at night when I find myself
Walking behind a woman alone on a deserted street

And I become aware she's becoming aware

Of me behind her, I'm moving in a straight line and she's not so of course
I'm within a few feet of her within seconds

Making me threatening, I could be anybody, some madman wanting

To kick something into her stomach, I soften
My steps so she won't have to hear them but this makes me even more threatening

So finally I move past her without looking and let her see

I'm just a harmless Asian dude, me smiling, I can almost feel myself

Patting this guy on the back.

SOMETIME SWEEP

I

Never mundane, the Brooklyn Bridge
Swivels through sunlight, spokes going, a stone soaring

While I sit half-asleep on the D train
Wobbling through Robert Musil, wavering in and out of the same sentence

Suddenly Ulrich saw the   Suddenly Ulrich   Suddenly Ulrich saw the whole
   thing in the

Rocking in rhythm with the other sleepers, the slumped, the shrunkfaces
Slivering open at the mouth
                         comical light of the question

Trying to pull myself out of the suck
Of sleep, an "epic, comic struggle," as a teacher of mine once put it, in words
   not exactly like that

II

              there was certainly an abundance

A Bridge glimpse through girders
Picks my head up a little
                              of mind around

                    other half-conscious heads tilting towards it

The Bridge is a statement, always flexing across the river

Always stalwart ambition
                                posed beyond the flickering

Girders, graffiti, D train going the opposite direction
Girders flashing like extra lashes on eyes that can't go wide enough to take in
    all of it

III

This is the best homage to the Bridge, the natural prayer
Of sleepy heads turning towards it, offering the tribute of what they have left

Of their attention
                      the only thing wrong was
                                          dimmed minds
Briefly firing
            the only thing wrong was that
                                          the distance

Between themselves and the Bridge like a physical regret

                the only thing wrong was

The distance between
                mind itself
                        what they could have been,
                                            was
What they still, possibly, could be
                devoid of mind
                                and now

    the only thing wrong was that mind itself was devoid of mind

IV

What's happened to you, mild man, what have you become

He was himself, after all

You used to attack books like this you used to mow them down
Now you sit repositioning your pants loathing that guy's thigh for touching yours

He was himself

What happened to your day-by-day determination
To work through the world's volumes to build up the stamina to match me

        one of those specialists who had renounced responsibility

Crane walked me, Mayakovsky walked me
                for the larger questions

V

The Brooklyn Bridge requires a total poetry

Never nods off never makes itself feel better by looking at the Manhattan or
    Williamsburg Bridge dozing

Never resents the East River
For lapping against it, the millions of overweight people for walking all over it,
The guided tours with their caesurae
Of historical morsels, the joggers jouncing it, pollocking their sweat

The water bottles brimming over its trash cans,
Scuttling its planks, the bicyclists superciliously moving through them flaring
    their messenger bags

The bad poetry thrown at it daily, the cantos of crap,
Young poets climbing its cables at midnight to feel gusts they can't summon
 at their computers

VI

The Brooklyn Bridge never manages
Its website, never shops online for patio furniture at Kmart,
Never explodes at the handle
Of a mini barbecue grill from Target for failing to screw on properly,
Never dreams of coming face-to-face
With Samsung customer service to give them a piece of its mind

VII

The Brooklyn Bridge never gives away pieces of its mind

Always a braining
      He was the less visible
           fire
             of the two
Always braiding
     searching for
         cathedrals of conveyance

Always mustering
     a possible handle to grasp
           never muttering

Never merely, never flinching
      the real mind of the mind
           always

A braining fire

IN PASSING WITH MY MIND ON NOTHING IN THE WORLD BUT THE RIGHT OF WAY I ENJOY BY VIRTUE OF THE LAW

after William Carlos Williams

In passing with my mind on nothing
In passing with my mind on

In passing with my mind on nothing in the world but the
Nothing

In passing with my mind on the world
I mind my nothing

In passing by my mind I enjoy the right nothing
In passing by the nothing I enjoy my mind on

In passing by the world I mind the right way
In passing by the way I enjoy the world

In passing my mind on I right the world
In passing my mind on I enjoy right of world

In passing nothing on I enjoy
My passing

In passing with nothing on I enjoy the law
In passing with virtue on I enjoy nothing in my mind

In passing by virtue
I enjoy the way of the world of the mind

By the way I mind my passing
I enjoy nothing

TO LEBRON'S ELBOW

I, too, sometimes go numb. I'm numb now,
    deadened all over my apartment on the day after
the Chosen One crooked you by His side
    on national television to announce His decision
to kill Cleveland, which somebody, ESPN
    or one of the Chosen One's "Team" or perhaps
the Chosen One Choosily Himself, named
    the Decision, with no irony at all, thus branding
a ready, snappy, definite-articled name to go
    alongside other such Cleveland catastrophes,
the Drive, the Fumble, the Shot, the Move,
    or in Rust Belt French, the LeBacle,
the Chosen One's maddening subtraction
    of Himself from the Cavs' historic, i.e. paralyzing,
Game 5 loss *at home* to the effing Boston Celtics
    in the 2010 Eastern Conference Semifinals,
a team He hammered at home in the playoffs
    two years earlier with that massive dunk over KG's head
that you helped author, when the Celtics
    were younger and fresher, eventual champions,
and the Chosen One had a far less supportive
    supporting cast. What the hell happened to Him in Game 5?
He looked out of joint, to say the least, loitering
    outside the three-point line while the Celtics drew
further away and the non-chosen panicked,
    nonplussed as to why He wasn't demanding the ball
and ramming it down Paul Pierce's fatfish face.
    Only the most important game of the season
and, in retrospect, the history of the Cavs franchise,
    and there was the Chosen One touching you
instead of the basketball, as if petting His own tentativeness,
    saying it was okay. After the game, fresh from
fuming on the subway ride home listening to too much

    Rage Against the Machine, feeling capable
of dismembering another person for the first time,
    specifically Rajon Rondo, I opened your Twitter page
and saw that you had checked to see if the Chosen
    Balls were still attached and could report that they were,
but "oddly singing showtunes." This didn't help,
    blaming His Balls instead of taking any
responsibility, just the fact that I was scouring
    your Twitter page shows how ridiculous everything
had become after we were all witnesses to no less
    than the withdrawal of a god followed by His press
conference afterward, at which He acted as if nothing strange
    had happened, saying you felt fine and that everyone
overreacted to one bad game because He "spoiled"
    people with His play. I wanted to see fury,
the same fury He unleashed on top of KG's head
    directed at Himself as He admitted His failure,
how He Himself was to blame for the loss,
    not His teammates or coach; but of course
this would have been a staggering admission
    on His part, accepting sole blame for the first time
in His career, saying, Yes, I now have the players
    around Me to win a championship, but I came up
against the moment of My greatness and I failed.
    In fact, I took the moment off. I was in la la land.
"Every career has a tipping point when you have to pour
    cement on the foundation," Bill Simmons says,
and the Chosen One was flinching under the first
    plops of that cement, coaxing open His own narrative
umbrella to shield Himself from the hardening
    of other men's judgment: I of course was pouring
it on, saying there was no way He could leave
    Cleveland after this, that He'd never live down
the embarrassment of quitting on the Cavs
    in the playoffs only to quit the entire city;
but even as I thought this I knew it was false,
    of course He could leave, of course He could live

down the embarrassment, if He went on to win
	multiple championships somewhere else He'd be
remembered for those, not for His failures;
	He could rewrite crapping out on Cleveland
as the inevitable discharge of crappy coaching
	and teammates; He could submit He'd taken
His hometown franchise as far as it could go
	before banging His elbow on the ceiling; yes,
He could work you in there, slyly, after a couple
	of championships, sitting down with Jim Gray again
propped by charity children, smiling and sipping
	from His **vitamin**water and admitting that, yes,
you were bothering Him more than He let on,
	but let's just leave it at that, Jim. I can see all this
playing out in His mind on the court as you went
	numb, feeding that slim fissure of doubt
into His feeling of invincibility, worming in
	the weft of the new narrative; perhaps there was
a twinge of regret as He felt something in Him
	diminished; but quickly that was buried
in His mind as He dug His new, wider foundation.
	And what did anyone expect? The "keenest
of human torments is to be judged without a law,"
	Camus writes in *The Fall*, and all of us (even you)
construct narratives to ease ourselves out
	of judgment, slip its prim stranglehold
on our identities; naturally, someone thinking of Himself
	as the "Chosen One" is not going to stand by
and be Prufrocked, "pinned and wriggling on the wall,"
	as everyone with a Twitter account (even you)
tells Him He is this or that but never going to be
	anything else, without maneuvering in whatever
way He can to spring Himself out of history
	into possibility again, even if that means giving up
His Chosen identity; after all, haven't I moved
	to New York to spring free of certain
judgments I now call "small town," haven't I

    (along with my chorus from Cleveland) damned LeBron
out of a desire to resurrect my own ruined narrative
    from the cement pour of His Last Judgment
aka the Decision? He's stupid, he's cruel, he's breathtakingly
    narcissistic, lost, a coward, a quitter, all ways
of scooping up some of that cement and dumping it
    back on him. But while the war is still on
for LeBron James's narrative, as he marshals his forces
    in Miami to shatter our attempts to set him,
the narrative for Cleveland has been cast,
    the city subsiding into its own cynicism again,
hardening into more poor history, this time
    through the masturbation of a television special;
and all I can do to feel free of that cast
    is to run my writing hands over its contours,
rub some feeling into me as LeBron tried
    to do with you, leave an imprint on how I'm being
shaped, showing I'm not completely useless,
    so were an actual god to come along at the end
of the game and need me to raise His right
    hand, He wouldn't have to switch to His left.

CONTENTS TEND TO SHIFT DURING FLIGHT

Are you a pretzel person or a peanut person?
    Someone asked me this once, I can't remember who,
or where I was going, we were on a plane,

    the stewardesses were shifting down the aisle
their cart of refreshments, one fore, one aft,
    doing their little duet of pop cans, plastic cups,

ice cubes and branded napkins, singing, *Something
    to drink?* from window to aisle, aisle to window,
tray tables unlatched and steadied row by row,

    almost a domino effect, people clearing papers
and magazines and paperbacks from their lap
    space, some rousing themselves from sleep,

grateful not to have been passed over, all poised
    to make their choice, Coke, Sprite, tomato juice,
ginger ale, accepting the foil pouch of pretzels

    or peanuts, sometimes getting to choose
between the two, hence the question, as if my identity
    depended on it, pretzel person, peanut person,

morning person, night person, cat person, dog person,
    Democrat, Republican, Christian, Muslim—
I don't like to think of myself in these terms.

    But people go to war over these choices, they
"fight over peanuts"; and I know I have to choose sides
    at times to participate in this weird menagerie

called civilization, if only to get some pretzels or peanuts,
    Coke or Sprite. The man who asked this question,
the answer was deeply important to him, he wanted

    to define himself for the duration of the trip,
if not his whole life, by his choice of one of two
    arbitrary salty options, he wanted to step into his choice

and be completely content with it, no regrets, no
    pining after peanuts with pretzels in his mouth,
and he seemed a little sorry for me when I said

    I had no idea, that I hadn't really thought about it.
I've always been between identities; with peanuts
    and pretzels it is no different, I could go either way

depending on my mood; I've spent more time thinking
    about my choice of drinks on planes, not wanting to be
stuck with something I'll have to throw down in shots

    once the stewardess comes guilting me down the aisle
with her trash bag. Now, after so many plane trips,
    I can safely say I'm a "ginger ale person," I waste no time

deliberating over other drinks; and I can see what
    the man was getting at, this just being *me*, decisively,
all the time, knowing all my material manifestations.

    Yet despite his passion to define himself through pretzels
or peanuts, I don't remember him or his choice
    but the question, just as all the meticulous ways

I've defined myself over the years have dropped away
    leaving me only with questions about the kind of person
I really am, as I continue to define myself with so many

      new means at my disposal, MySpace, Facebook,
Twitter, all of which will disappear or be replaced
      in ten years leaving me clutching at something

else. The choice between peanuts and pretzels
      is gone. Most airlines today can't afford even one
of these options. You might hear this as a rebuke

      of the man's question, proof that we should be asking
something more important—Are you a good person
      or a bad person?—but somehow the question keeps

coming back to me, I hear it every time I get on a plane;
      and I remember, a month after 9/11, when
I was flying to see someone I felt serious enough about

      to fly during that time, whom later I would choose
another, younger woman over just as she had chosen
      me over another, older man, waking up to the sound

of pop cans popping open and being poured
      furious over ice, the stewardesses extending drinks
and divvying pretzels and peanuts with more care,

      more hunger to help, as if they knew there was something
sacred in this, that these stupid little liberties in the air,
      these peanuts, were what we most wanted to protect.

II

SELF-INSTALLATION

>   *after* The Letters of Vincent Van Gogh

It seemed less and less like eating strawberries in spring.
Less the blue buildings in the morning, more the beige
Of afternoon. You like beige, she said, brown
And beige. He looked around the room. More the bore
Walls of the mean room, less beyond the head, less
Instead of, I paint infinity, less the Yes possible,
Soft yes of kiss upon kiss, more the slight fadedness,
Sex gotten through, sex as exercise, all I excised,
Cleaning dishes right after dinner to put off the dread.
Less recklessness. Less wrecking, more reckoning,
More wreckage in the reckoning. Less she and no other,
More another and another, less logic, more logic,
Less against all logic, who is the master, the logic or I,
Is the logic there for me or am I there for the logic,
Is there no reason, no sense, in this unreasonableness,
This lack of sense? Less sense in more sense. The sentence.
Less activity in the looking, begging the brushwork
Out of the body, the God out of the body, getting the got
Out. More rinsing, more ironing, more soap. More stunned.
Less love as nothing rather than, love as exactness, this
Exactly what I want to be doing, nothing I would rather be
Doing, this here, this now, this coffee with autumn with you.
Less loosening, less lessening. More of more of more.

WHAT WE TALK ABOUT WHEN WE TALK ABOUT

I thought I should write this down, since your ear
is a vagina and you might not hear it if I said it out loud,
she wrote, and I couldn't tell if she was being sweet
or funny or was just angry with me, mostly I was confused
by the metaphor and thought it was a little extreme,
I mean, was a vagina the first thing that came to mind
when she thought of my ear? Which ear was she talking about?
By then I was fingering my right ear thinking it wasn't
all that different from a vagina, I wouldn't be so shocked
if I took off her pants and saw an ear where her vagina
should be, took off her hat and saw two vaginas
where her ears should be, ears and vaginas were closer
than, say, vaginas and toes, and she often caressed
my ear with her tongue the way one might caress
a vagina, I'm not saying I climaxed but the possibility
was there. I looked back at previous messages between us
and saw one saying "I have a cat's vagina for an ear,"
which briefly clarified things until it didn't: a cat's vagina?
Somehow there was context for this, possibly we were
laughing about saying "a pussy's pussy" in bed,
or I was laughing about it while she and my large male cat
regarded me with some rather serious reservations,
in any case going back in time translating phrase to phrase
didn't make things any clearer, let alone cleaner,
between us, cats and ears and vaginas were coming
to stand for our entire relationship! We'd never developed
a vocabulary for tenderness, I saw, which was hurting us
now that she wanted to say how she really felt,
or at least felt it was time to say how she really felt,
one day before the new year. On New Year's Day
I woke up early to rinse all the extra glasses we'd used
for our party, careful not to clink them too much
as she slept facedown on the bed, still in her little black

dress, her long, cool jewelry tangled in her hair.
I started packing, jamming sweaters and socks
and scarves into my suitcase, and when she finally
pushed herself off her pillow, looking everywhere but at me,
I put on her Peruvian hat, posing in her earflaps
and braids, and she said, You're covering your vaginas.

LUNCH SPECIAL

How quickly the old sadness comes back.
You strewn on a chair eating lunch
    alone, fat meatball parm
    slagged in front of you, book & notebook

    replaced by a phone. One other
couple in the restaurant, fanny-packed tourists
    pestering the waitress
    about biking the Brooklyn Bridge, No,

    but, what we mean is, Can we bike in this city
without a helmet? Nothing stirring
    but a vague desire
    to pluck one of Citibank's new blue rental bikes

    off the mechanized rack outside
and ride the Bridge yourself, looking for some
    healing transport, some
    speed back to a wider, lighter selfhood,

    no cynicism about the Citibike
program, no regarding the rack an intrusion
    into "your" neighborhood,
    no judging the tourists stupid, needing to have

    their unhelmeted heads bashed in
by the bikes, but believing only in the blue
    slicing through
    the sunlit crowds congregating in the sky,

    a soloist's note separating
the rest, launching ahead stupidly
    unprotected, capable
    of such huge, stupid questions

       that return it, in the end, to this table
unfed, stumped in solitude, so why bother?
              You are already there,
       here. And in truth you didn't think

       of biking across the Bridge,
only added that thought as you set yourself
              to thinking seriously
       about your sadness. Every time

       the waitress comes to ask
if you're okay, your face is full of parm,
              stuffed goon, and you think
       she must be a bored god just fucking with you

       on a random afternoon, Beckett himself
couldn't script her timing any better,
              the whole room evacuated
       of even the tourists now, just you,

       your sandwich and your phone,
the waitress materializing from the wings
              to iron you over
       in spotlight, just as soon withdrawing

       as you nod, trying to eke out
a yes, the chorus of chairs around you
              silent, the windows,
       the bikes, the city. Your face is full of pain

       you chew and swallow so genteelly
in napkined-over bites, steering helmeted
              down this familiar
       back alley, gripping the handlebars

    of sandwich and phone, none
the wiser, all too imperious, thinking somehow
            you can get away
        with this, clenching and squinting.

ORPHEUS ON LEXINGTON AVENUE

Sometimes she isn't even beautiful, just a girl
with a youthful waist or finely sculpted legs,
but still he has to turn and catch a fuller glimpse
of her, afraid that if he doesn't study her
a second time he might miss some crucial
encounter, a singing in the body he hasn't
yet heard. If he can't possess it, he tells himself,
he should at least be aware of its possibility.

So he walks alone through the darkening city
to meet his wife uptown, haunted by strangers
passing into great unclaimed rooms, offering him
a life more delirious, until he feels so caught
up in them that everyone, even Eurydice,
is disappearing, lost in his pursuit of the nameless.

FIRST SONG

after Stan Getz & Kenny Barron

He stands in the kitchen, listening to the song
    cut through the washing of dishes, hands softly
        sponging routinely as he turns and looks back

over his shoulder at the music, as if expecting
    to see something there, some pain embodied in
        the perforations of the speakers, the still spines

of the books in back of them trembling, Getz himself
    emerging out of the attentive air to blow his last
        great ballad in Copenhagen, crouched on

a bar stool by the piano to prop his weakening body
    with more support, the cancer infiltrating his liver,
        gaining on him with each new breath he bequeaths

to the song reaped by the man now twenty years later,
    wondering what to do with such late opulence
        of sound, trying to feel something appropriate,

to summon some hurt to match this princely lament,
    some figure from his past to focus on who trained him
        in the acoustics of heartbreak; but everything

blurs inside him as he stands there, his hands still
    moving the sponge in a circle around the plate
        as if around the click wheel of the iPod

pouring the music, his mind scrolling through moments
    and faces as if through the thousands of digitized songs
        he can thumb through now without thinking,

though once they were the world, his whole past
        in his pocket, archived in clean, cool, alphabetical
                compartments, more available than ever

but somehow sealed off, leaving him stranded in sound
        self to preside over his small empire of identity;
                unable to remember the last time he felt any real

loneliness or longing, as when he first fell in love
        with Getz's music and lay in bed for hours pawing
                at the sound, solos filling and refilling him

with distances; unable even to long for that longing,
        so far beyond the first fires, knowing how innocent
                that unbearable time was, how much hidden

pleasure was in it, how you didn't lose your innocence
        the first time someone surprised you with great pain
                but when you saw yourself capable of causing

that same pain in another, and were untouched.

THE FUTURE ROOM

after Blue Valentine

In the Future Room, every time the robot clock
Says "6:30," it sounds like "sex party." So you get up
Thinking, Come again? I have to come again?
Coming's become hard again, though your genitals
Are mostly synthetic and governed by the time
Release of pills. You have to think through the Rolodex
Of images in your mind to find a girl who looks
Organic enough to excite you. You find an unlikely
Source of arousal in the image of the Rolodex
Itself, so quaint with its little white flipping cards.
Your partner, sadly, can see right through you,
As all your innermost thoughts glow visible
On the LCD screen cut into your forehead.
She finds you livelier than the Reality Classics
Syndicated on TV, touched by those moments
When her own image pops up on the LCD,
By how hard you try to fix her there while working
To a climax, thinking of the first time you saw her,
Imagining her showering with her Australian
Tennis instructor when she was fifteen, still virgin.
But inevitably your mind clicks on some human
Girl you used to have real sex with, back in the days
When you couldn't just have sex with anybody
By friending them on Fukbook, the revolutionary
Virtual sex networking site that finally ended
The hegemony of Facebook. You always focus
On her flaws, the way she looked old sometimes
In the morning, the mole between her breasts,
Her deviated septum. All those things you thought
You gave up for good when suddenly you could
Have sex with more and more perfect creatures

With no strings, no STDs attached, coming came
So easily until you were coming so constantly
Coming became not coming, not coming became
Orgasmic, oh the old days fantasizing about someone,
Stuck concocting some shabby, softcore scenario
In your head while fiddling with your old, frequently
Flaccid penis, or sitting in the kitchen with her
Sharing an omelet in your frayed robes, feeling
Weirdly sad and guilty that you weren't having
As much sex with her as you used to, who knows
Why, but mostly happy, you think, mostly happy.

THE SOUND

    Slowly

                    People   go

               silent.

        I have long dreamed
                                in dull play.

      is this pain come near me?
      I thought my heart would burst,

                raw water
                   and fleshy embers.

Now

       cold work of books and stones.

I

   burn

And spear my heart's

   cover

And depart unhurt.

                erasure of Ashbery's "Eclogue"

CLOSE EMBRACE

for Robin Thomas

The embrace always feels great at the beginning,
    but then you take a few steps
  and it falls apart. You're tall, she's small.
      Try not to stoop.
    The wind keeps blowing the tarp off

  the patio table. You go out,
    clamp it down, no way the wind
      gets in there now.
    But the wind finds a way. Rust creeps
up the legs of the patio chairs. Funny how

    you stood so long at Kmart,
internally debating the merits of chairs.
      As if you could
        buy one set and be finished with
the chair chapter of your life—an ass

    finds ways of warping what once
seemed firm. Every tanda is a conversation.
      First dance, Hello.
    Second dance, Oh, I love that show.
Third dance, You used to be an artist?

      Huh. I like art.
  Or first dance, Wow, you're really into
      your education. Second dance,
Do you always talk this much about your shoes? Third
    dance, Thanks, I need some absinthe.

With one dancer you can do no wrong,
 with another,
  bruises on the ankles. You're
   never as far from middle school
as you think. Never a master, finished and free.

∞

You thought yourself advanced, then
 danced with her and felt the thousands
of other dances in her body,
 the listening
lightness of her embrace, schooled by so many long

 milongas, days and nights spent making
  small adjustments
  to other bodies, attending
to the labor of variables, height, width, weight,
  smell, style, school, attitude,

  floor size, speed, columns, crowdedness,
   stiletto heel suddenly
    spiking her out
of nowhere, skill level of other dancers on
  the floor, all the judging eyes looking

 on, tempo and temperament
of music, texture and temperature
 of skin, clothing, sweat on the palm
  and forehead: all
of which allowed her to feel even the slightest

 stiffness in your movements, the slightest
uncertainty or imprecision, the slightest
  need to show off,
  responding only to a true
  lead, not things choreographed

    in a class, hearing even
your subtlest intentions and echoing them
            back as form, the ideal reader
            made flesh, showing
    you glimmerings of the ideal in

            how far you were from the ideal,
    demonstrating that this is always
            a limitless
practice, endless variations of each movement,
        endless variations in

            and out of each
    movement, to dance to revel in, not
            despair over, such endlessness,
        relinquishing perfection
for again and again and again and again.

∞

    The students are working on
            their new moves, boleos, ganchos,
colgadas, volcadas, preferring the flashy
        stuff to mere walking, some so clumsy
            you wonder why

    they're bothering to take dance classes
        at all, why, if they persist,
            they don't just try to master the
basics first. They're learning to speak a new language,
            but unlike what

        they would do were they learning Greek,
    German or French, getting a grasp of
the alphabet, pronunciation, building up
        a vocabulary of
            simple, useful

words to put together in simple,
        useful phrases
like *Hey, how's it going?* or *Where is the bathroom?*
    they try to say the hardest words
  first, without bothering to

    learn the appropriate context
in which to use them or even what they express,
    sounding more ridiculous
      the more they try
  to impress. The teacher moves around

    the room, stressing
the importance of fundamentals, comparing
  tango to martial arts, where you drill
    the simplest things repeatedly,
  he says, because in tango,

    if you screw up, nothing happens,
  but in martial arts, you die.
    The students laugh,
then go on forcing their way through to what they think
  is advancement, not wanting to be

branded a beginner on the dance floor, trying
      to learn new steps
    by skipping the steps, to put on
    the fragrance of form without
the foundation. The teacher smiles, shakes

    his head a little and scans this
      room of mumblers
he's created, wincing at the guy
    who keeps trying to say *ca-*
*nard, ca*nard! to every bewildered follower,

wanting to tell him you cannot lie
    in tango, especially
to a woman who can say *echolalia*
        effortlessly with her feet. What,
            he wants to ask,

        is the rush? Why this constant need
            to acquire
newer, flashier moves? Sometimes he
wonders what everyone is after in tango,
        what learning a boleo

or gancho translates into—social status? Sex?
        Maybe the men
            think, as he did once, that learning
            these moves will gain them access
to the women they've always wanted

        to meet, even if just to touch
            them, briefly, in an embrace;
but what they'll soon find out is that no matter how
        beautiful the woman, how close
            the embrace, once

        you begin dancing the form is
            always between
you, you're always dancing with the form
as much as the woman, so that it's possible
        to feel when you leave the floor

        that you really haven't touched her
at all, haven't just held in your arms
        that body you coveted
so keenly from across the room and finally
        worked up enough

            courage to confront; possible,
      even, that you didn't enjoy it,
because she can't follow all of your leads or is
                so much better
         than you that you feel her bored

                or judging you
      in the embrace, making you begin
           to think screwing up is not just
making a mistake, but making nothing happen;
        and so the dance feels empty.

          But you can't fill this emptiness
      with more gibberish, flying
    from one new partner to another;
the only way to feel something happening is
           to feel the floor

      beneath you as you dance, anchoring
              the weight of where
you're going to where you are, slowing yourself down
          to feel your partner's weight as you
      work with her to coalesce

              in weightless form—
    which is what you remember, he thinks,
        stamping out time for his students
      with his feet, not the beauty
of a body, but what you made between you, how

            you disappeared.

I'LL FOLLOW YOU

It is sweet to kiss the ear of your kitty
as he sleeps. Sweet to pull the high-top sneakers

off your girlfriend's feet as she sleeps.
Sweet to discover she is not completely asleep

by the way she lifts her second foot a little
to make the untying easier. Sweet to wake up

to the sound of her silence in the bathroom
as she readies herself for work, touching up her face

as gently as your kitty laps water from his bowl.
At these times you don't question anything,

what is love, whether you're working hard
enough, whether you're not missing something

somewhere else. Life couldn't be elsewhere.
She comes to kiss you goodbye and rests her head

on your chest for a moment, so sweet to pretend
you're asleep through this, sweet to listen to her

walk out your door remembering to lock it,
sweet through the hall, sweet through the second

door, through the gate, the sweet of the latch,
sweet imagining the singular sounds she makes

as she moves through the rest of her day.
So sweet you don't ask how to reconcile all this

with what sweetness you feel alone after she leaves.

EMPIRE

Warm days I sat outside, enjoying the concrete.
The tilting chain-link fences, one strung up
With rope. The rocky soil, what was left
After my scorched-earth campaign wiped out
The weeds. The aboriginal weeds, hip-high,
Sometimes neck-high fuckers that took two hands
To free. Hard to believe such things could come
Out of that earth, which when I planted basil
Turned up chunks of rock, glass, paper, plastic,
Even some rubber balls. It wouldn't give
Beyond two feet; my shovel edged and stopped
Against some prehistoric rock. I grew
Three basil plants in the middle of the yard,
Watering them religiously, coaxing
Them through their first few fragile weeks, until
They flourished in the summer sun and looked
—Like weeds. I didn't think about this much,
Just kept killing any upstart weeds
I saw threatening the yard. I took strange pride
In this, creating the image of my order
Against the backdrop of Robert Moses's
Expressway cutting through the neighborhood.
Moses saw the homes and businesses
On 3rd Avenue as weeds. Then his plant raged
Into a weed, feeding on everything
Left standing, until the State, sixty years
Later, decided finally to think
Of ways to clear it that would grow more green
Off the land. "That's going to be a tunnel,"
My next-door neighbor, Ishmael, said to me
One night, pointing at the expressway. I found
This hard to believe. "You should buy your place.
These properties along the freeway are cheap,

And going to be worth a lot more money."
All the subtle powers at work I knew
So little about, tunneling under the ground
My efforts couldn't crack, contending for
Empire: the State, the real estate investors,
The weeds, the ants steadily colonizing
The yard, sending swarmers through a hole
In my bathroom: and every morning I
Woke up and planted my identity
So firmly on the floor, stamping it through
The rooms so carefully articulated
With my possessions, calmly making myself
A cappuccino with a new machine
And peering hatefully at my backyard neighbor,
Who blasted his bachata all day long
And thought he could just come into my yard,
Dig up the dirt and knock down the wall
Between us, leaving all the rubble piled
On my side—which he could, because what say
Did I have in the matter? I was just
A colonist on some other powers' land,
And even if I owned the place, like Ishmael
Did his, it wouldn't really be *mine*, as his
Place wasn't *his*, connected as it was
To other structures like my landlord's, which
Was falling apart (to his indifference), and
Bachata boy's backyard, which was turning
Into some kind of dance plantation louder
Than the expressway; which is why, when I
Went to stop the digging, I stood there soft
On softer, heaped-up earth just watching him
Ignore me, studying how he curtly worked
The ground, scooping up what looked like a skull
But was the plastic head of a coffee maker.
Poor Mr. Coffee, buried who knows when,
Or how, by (or with?) what lordly tenant,

Who once walked these grounds as assuredly
As me, grounds as shifting as the grounds
He packed each day into his machine, then dumped
The next blank morning to make way for more.

THE CONTINUING STRUGGLE OF THE PHILISTINES JR.

> *Hey, hey, it's the end of the world again*
> *Here we are just waiting for everything to end*
> —The Philistines Jr.

I

We're somewhere in South Carolina, I think on Folly Beach,
Where we threw a football once, you and I,
I the quarterback and you the wide receiver, we couldn't stop laughing
At "wide receiver." You kept diving to catch my passes,
Trying to hit the inside of a cresting wave
Just as the ball arrived. I liked treating you like
The younger brother I never had, eating dinner alongside you on our couch
While we watched TV
Instead of breaking out the fancy napkins
And looking at you across the kitchen table, as I did the first night
We had sex.
How could I resist those napkin rings? you said.
Hey, it only took the end of the world for me to regret this, to remember
How I also treated my younger sister, making her do slant routes
In our upstairs hallway at home in Pepper Pike,
Where errant passes knocked crystals off Mom's chandelier.

II

Hey, it's the end of the world again.
The sky looks scratched, like an old vinyl record
Played too many times then forgotten about, used
As a makeshift coaster, a coffee table
Conversation starter. You never used the real coasters
I set out, just dumped your drinks
Wherever you damn pleased, including on top of my only Billy Joel record.

I'm not so mad about that anymore,
Just as I'm not so mad at all the planes that keep dumping their mugs of jet fuel
Wherever they please. The damned please.
Only a few planes left, even fewer peanuts on those planes, the once
    outrageously long lines
Have dwindled. I like the word "dwindled."
Antarctica has dwindled. But people keep flying there
While there's still a chance to see a whole continent melt. Or see at all.

III

It's the end of the world again
And you refuse to go anywhere. You figure you can
Keep up with what everyone else is doing
On Facebook. I'm looking at this plane taking off
And you're texting. It's the end of the world
And you're texting. You're also wearing cargo pants,
Which I deplore. I've got my hands on my hips;
Someone in the dunes behind us
Might be taking a picture of all this, an album cover for the final, vinyl sky,
And I want to show I've got nothing to do
With those cargo pants. Other people in the distance
Put their hands on their hips, but with much less
Authority, look at how they keep slipping their hands in their pockets,
Perhaps wishing they had cargo pockets.
I've learned a lot from sorority girls' Facebook photos.

IV

What else have I learned?
Oh, not much, how tastefully to underline my books,
How not to split infinitives, how to fit all my toiletries into one quart-size
    Ziploc bag.
More recently, how to make Rachael Ray's buttermilk chicken tenders
For Super Bowl Sunday. What joy to hear you refer to them as "chickens."

Are the chickens done yet? you asked from the couch.
And then you learned how to make seafood pasta, which you knew I loved,
And I almost died when I heard you say "shrimps."

HERE ARE YOUR WATERS AND YOUR WATERING PLACE

I love the way you make everything plural
I don't have any underwears left, you say in the morning
No, I don't count sheeps
You want to be as alive as possible meaning multiple even in your sleeps
One might be able to count sheep to sleep
But one can't count sheeps
Verbing all over the pasture, leaving
Ordure on the verdure
No, ordures on the verdures, you would say, they're dropping dungs
Teach me how to be less singular
Teach me how to open order to ordure
To orchards
I love how you leave waters all over the apartment
One by the couch one on the dining table two by the kitchen sink
I go past these glasses
And suddenly see how thirsty I was
How much of a desert my life is how much of a camel I've become

KISSING YOU

Is better than poetry, better than painting, better than baseball, Brooklyn Bridge
  walks, croissants with nutella,
Better than Proust, all six volumes, lingering longer, lush-slower,
Better than reading anything in the original French,
Better than Beethoven by Wilhelm Kempff, any last name ending in
Pff,
Better than the Philharmonious hair of Herbert von Karajan,
Better than the Tony Leung films in the oeuvre of Wong Kar Wai,
Better than the sound *oeuvre*, though this does come close to capturing that
  kissing-you sound,
Better than *Moby-Dick* the second time around,
Better than Mr. Pecksniff with muffin on his knee,
Better than the beautifully broomed blue suit tailored for me by Mr. Joe Hemrajani,
Better than bachata with Alessia Andrade,
Better than Beatrice and Benedick,
Better than birthday cards from Tyler: I like you and I love you, oh I love you,
  but my fish died,
Better than the intricately cut shoes of Pierre Corthay and much, much less
  expensive, in fact free,
Better than the simple, slim, unpretentious $1.50 cardboard MUJI notebooks
  I write about you in,
Better than Basquiat brooding with a cat in his lap,
Better than the chance meeting of a sewing machine and an umbrella on an
  operating table,
Kissing you is a slow-time manifesto,
Better than Brooklyn Lager after logging a long day of sloughing off teaching
  in the Bronx
And just *blowing away* English Composition, copy codes and department meetings,
Likewise burnt toast, rock-hard baguettes, balding and the BQE,
And let's not forget the DMV and the DMZ,
Better than Motoki working around my wobble as I fall half-asleep in his salon chair,
Better than postcoital orange Fanta, though we can include that too

Because you bring out the *J'adore* in me, when I think of you I want to come up with names for new perfumes,
Better than Grom hazelnut gelato, cool as a Stan Getz solo,
Better than a Stan Getz solo, though even better with one going in the background,
Better than Ben Webster's endless tenor shudderings leaving rose print on the spaces of the night,
Best with long, Ben Webster–filled late nights breathing in the bouquet behind you,
Better than Lester? Yes, better than Lester,
Though it's a tough call in the morning when we listen to him backing Lady Day,
Best not to choose, Why not take all of me? as Lady Day asks in the new voice of the world.

WORK

Every day Django goes to work at the same time.
Takes breakfast at eight, runs a quick shower-paw over the ears, then hits the office
By 8:25. And by office I mean
Bed. This is work he excels at, stretching and accepting
Petting when he's looking particularly cute. I find the word "particularly"
Particularly hard to say, but Anna has no such problems;
Every day she goes to work putting people into yoga poses, making them say "particularly"
With their bodies. In yoga, you learn to release yourself
By resisting yourself. What a beautiful idea.
Even more beautiful is how one almost always feels this actually to be happening while doing it,
Unlike poetry, which is governed by a similar idea
Yet rarely provides this feeling while one is doing it.
Of course, one never really feels oneself
To be "doing" it. Anna leaves a mat on the kitchen floor
That serves as a runway for spontaneous headstands
As I'm "writing." I'll be walking back and forth between Django's office and the kitchen
And think, Hell, let's get inverted.
Already today I've done three headstands.
Anna recommends this as a good way to get the blood
Pumping through the brain in the morning
And hence the poetry, but so far I have yet to see Rilkean results.
Django loves his work, he never tires of being tired.
It is a particularly human quality to grow tired of being tired.
Look at him using the whole country of the bed,
First camping out in Florida, Maine, Alaska, Mississippi, now Idaho, Oregon, Nebraska, Arizona.
He likes to spread the good work of his body around, as does
Anna, what a service she gives her students.
She makes them feel better about their bodies and themselves.
Importantly, her students want to be there.

I go to work in the Bronx and most often my students do not want to be there.
What a strange thing, to be required to be somewhere
You don't want to be, submitting yourself to the particularly painful torture
Of writing. They put up with it because the college demands it
And listening to the college will help them get a job.
I talk and they listen and don't listen and more and more
I wonder what I am doing. I am not making them feel better about themselves
    or their bodies
Like Anna, and I am certainly not making myself feel better
Like Django. Who wins? English Composition?
Django has moved to Pennsylvania, which is a big state but he covers almost
    all of it.
He's got his left rear white paw sticking out like a golf putter
Over the Warhol museum in Pittsburgh, where there's a wonderful room
Full of silver balloon pillows blowing around
Called *Silver Clouds*. That is one way to work.
You know you're making people happy when you're making clouds.
Warhol told Lou Reed he wasn't working hard enough,
But maybe Lou Reed just wanted to be making clouds and couldn't
Because ol' Factory Warhol had already smelled that idea out.
Warhol would also tell me I'm not working hard enough, to which I'd say,
You look like you have a cat on your head.
Does your cat think your head is his office? His paws give you all your ideas?
A little scratch or two and presto, Clouds. Many thanks, Fluffy.
Django provides no such service.
Amazing we've been together all these years and still he speaks no English.
I speak a little cat but he can't even say "Hi."
Since Anna moved in, Django no longer sleeps on the bed at night.
He sleeps in my office and I sleep in his office; in the morning, we change
    places to go to work.
Django had to cede position to Anna, the superior speaker of English and petter.
The problem with Django is he accepts all this petting
And never gives any back. That's just not part of his line of work.
Neither is playing the guitar without a full assortment
Of fingers, as his namesake Django Reinhardt could beautifully do.
Just once I'd like to feel him rub me on my belly.

Who speaks better English, Django or my students?
On some days, it's a toss-up. At least Django harbors no pretensions
He's good at English, unlike those students I have to strain
To give a C who storm into my office wondering why they haven't gotten an A.
I do feel bad for them, they accept all this torture,
No petting whatsoever. But they give the torture back.
I don't grade their papers so much as continually cry for help in a quicksand
    of sentences.
I'm trying to teach them how to write critical papers
So they can potentially write papers for any college course.
And so I prepare them for college but not for life.
If I were preparing them for life, I'd teach them how to write
Thoughtful, anger-alleviating breakup letters,
Sweet but sexy Valentine's Day cards,
Witty but grave toasts and eulogies that make everyone in the room want to
    sleep with you,
Tasteful, unburdensome thank-you notes,
And gracious but subtly snarky emails to hopelessly idiotic but higher-
    ranking coworkers.
I'm a writer. When have I actually used a thesis statement
In my adult life? Sometimes I think thesis statements were invented
To make reading student papers less onerous for teachers
Because they helped them identify the student's heretofore MIA main point.
But ironically students in search of a thesis statement
Have come to write particularly gruesome English.
Sometimes when I have trouble with the word "particularly"
I can hear a vestige of how my parents struggle with r and l sounds in English.
What a nightmare for a Korean speaker, all those r/l sounds
Jammed together in such a fast, polysyllabic word.
I remember how my mom used to pronounce the word "film"
Fihdum. I thought this was kind of cute actually.
But when my students make mistakes with the language
I go insane, and Anna has to hear about it as we detox after work at night
By intoxicating ourselves with beer or wine.
What a mystery, how one person learns and another doesn't.
Or maybe not a mystery. Every day my dad woke up early to work at the hospital.

We moved from Minneapolis to St. Paul to New York to Toledo to Cleveland
As he kept getting better and better jobs.
He worked hard to get better jobs so he could get paid enough
To send me to better schools, where I learned the particularly particular craft of English,
So someday I could release myself like this.

ACKNOWLEDGMENTS

Thanks to the editors of the following publications, in which earlier versions of these poems first appeared:

Barn Owl Review: "Model Minority"
The Brooklyn Rail: "Struck from the Float Forever Held in Solution," "Take Your Time"
Copper Nickel: "First Song"
DIAGRAM: "The Sound"
Diode: "The Continuing Struggle of the Philistines Jr.," "Sometime Sweep," "To LeBron's Elbow"
The Fiddleback: "Empire"
Fifth Wednesday: "Here Are Your Waters and Your Watering Place," "Self-Installation"
Jabberwock Review: "Contents Tend to Shift During Flight"
The Journal: "American Dream," "For Every Atom Belonging to Me," "Orpheus on Lexington Avenue"
La Petite Zine: "Sent Dad a Golf Trunk Organizer," "What We Talk About When We Talk About"
Loaded Bicycle: "Close Embrace"
Matter: "Lunch Special"
Mead: "In Passing with My Mind on Nothing in the World but the Right of Way I Enjoy by Virtue of the Law"
The Missouri Review: "I'll Follow You" (as "Do You Hear Me, Poison Ivy?"), "Work"
Octopus: "Giant Steps," "*GQ* Correspondence"
The Owls: "A Natural History of My Name"
The Pinch: "The Future Room"
Southeast Review: "America's Favorite Poem"
Vinyl Poetry: "Empty Orchestra"
The Yale Review: "Kissing You"

Thanks to *Verse Daily* for republishing "Model Minority," *Curlew Quarterly* for republishing "I'll Follow You" and *Schuylkill Valley Journal* for republishing "Struck from the Float Forever Held in Solution." Thanks to Tina Cane for selecting an excerpt from "Here Are Your Waters and Your Watering Place" to appear in Rhode Island buses as part of *Poetry in Motion*, Rhode Island.

Thanks to the Vermont Studio Center for a month-long residency deep in the blizzards of January 2010 that got this book off the ground.

Thanks to my poetry fam for your amazing work and friendship—there are far too many of you to name here. Special thanks to Terrance Hayes, David Hernandez and Dottie Lasky for the cover props and Jason Bredle, Steve Gehrke, Marc McKee and Taije Silverman for reading this book in manuscript and making it better. Thanks to Jake Adam York for all you did on this earth: we miss you.

Thanks to my family, Mom, Dad, Lily, Julie, Hank, Tyler, Alex, Luke, Ben, Mitch, Laerte, Zilda, Marcelo and Maria Luiza! I love you so much. Thanks to Larry and Patti Greenberg for being like family to me in Brooklyn. Thanks to Anna Greenberg for your inspiration, love, and endurance, which brought this book to life.

Thanks to Trent Thibodeaux for the beautiful cover and John Estes for the meticulous interior design of the original edition. Thanks to Joe and Wendy Pan and everyone at Brooklyn Arts Press for the great work that you do and for giving this book a second life.

Thanks to Django (rest in peace) and the Brooklyn Bridge. Thanks to my original Brooklyn Poets fam, Tiffany Gibert, Caroline Gonzalez and Gunny Scarfo, for helping me build the poetry community I never had in Brooklyn while writing the poems in this book. Thanks to my soul sisters Simone Muench and Nicky Beer for always being there. Thanks to my boys B. C. Hughes, Bobby Thor Liddell and Gadzooks Bernard—in the original acknowledgments, I said "let's get to effing Maine already," but now I've been there with Ana Maria so let's pick another place to get together again.

Thanks to Ana Maria for saying yes at sunset on that beautiful day by the Portland Head Light. So much light has come into my life because of you.

ABOUT THE AUTHOR

Named one of the "100 Most Influential People in Brooklyn Culture" by *Brooklyn Magazine*, Jason Koo is the author of the poetry collections *More Than Mere Light*, *America's Favorite Poem* and *Man on Extremely Small Island*. Coeditor of the *Brooklyn Poets Anthology*, he has published his poetry and prose in the *American Scholar*, *Missouri Review*, *Village Voice* and *Yale Review*, among other places, and won fellowships for his work from the National Endowment for the Arts, Vermont Studio Center and New York State Writers Institute. An associate teaching professor of English at Quinnipiac University, Koo is the founder and executive director of Brooklyn Poets and creator of the Bridge (poetsbridge.org). He lives in Brooklyn.

www.ingramcontent.com/pod-product-compliance
Lightning Source LLC
LaVergne TN
LVHW040157080526
838202LV00042B/3209